12.89

THE
APARTMENT
HOUSE TREE

THE
APARTMENT
HOUSE TREE

Bette Killion

illustrated by
Mary Szilagyi

Harper & Row, Publishers

Library of Congress Cataloging-in-Publication Data
Killion, Bette.
   The apartment house tree / by Bette Killion : illustrated by Mary
Szilagyi.
      p.   cm.
   Summary: Describes how a tall tree at the edge of the woods can
provide living space for a multitude of animals, including squirrel,
woodpecker, tree frog, beetle, and raccoon.
   ISBN 0-06-023273-0 : $. — ISBN 0-06-023274-9 (lib. bdg.) :
$
   1. Forest fauna—Juvenile literature.   2. Trees—Juvenile
literature. [1. Trees.   2. Animals—Habitations.   3. Forest
ecology. 4. Ecology.]   I. Szilagyi, Mary, ill.   II. Title.
QL112.K55   1989   88-35700
591.5'2642—dc19   CIP
                                                       AC

1 2 3 4 5 6 7 8 9 10
First Edition

To all my grandchildren:
        Amy, Jeff, Andrew, Brad, Joe,
        Michael, Miriam, Ryan, Megan
        —and especially Adele
                B.K.

                To my parents
                        M.S.

In a plump, tall tree
at the edge of the woods,
many families live hidden away.

On the first floor,
a bushy-tailed squirrel and his wife
crack nuts with their sharp, pointed teeth.

Around the corner,
a prickly porcupine finds a vacant apartment
and decides she and her baby will move right in.

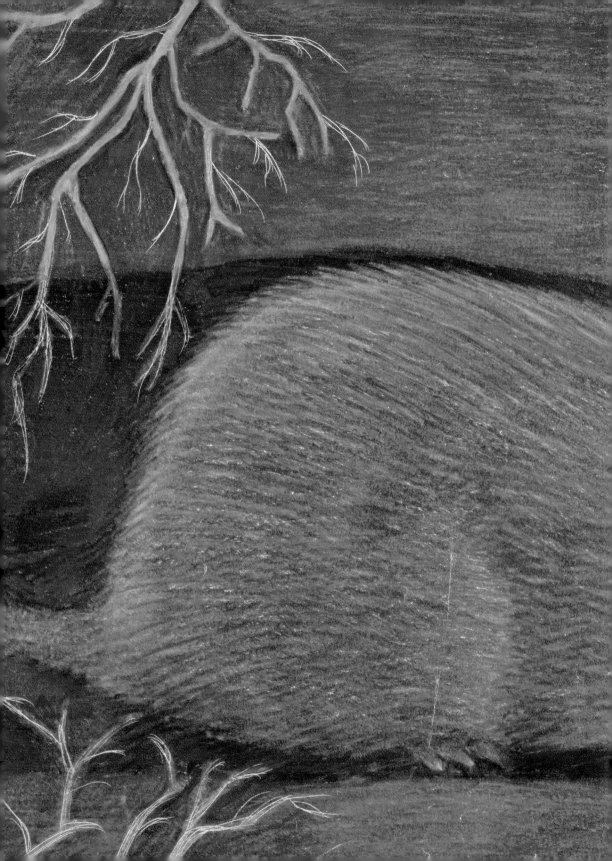

In the basement,
the mole has tunneled
quiet, dark rooms among the roots.

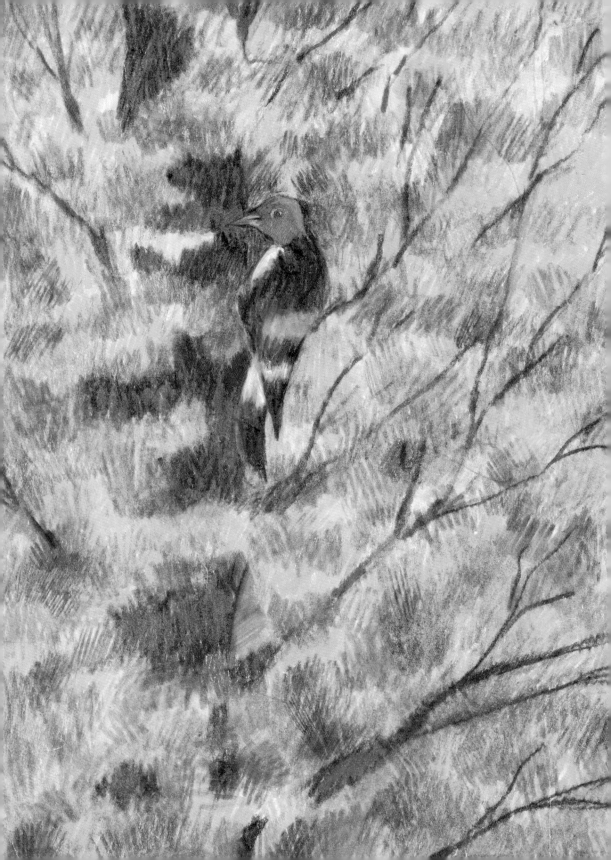

High on the tree trunk,
a red-headed woodpecker is busy
with his long, sturdy beak,
carving a room of his own.

Upstairs,
snuggled into its nest on a leafy branch,
lives a family of hummingbirds.

Higher still, in a small, round hole,
the ruffle-feathered owl is tucked away,
sleeping the day through.

An orange and green tree frog
clasps his long toes around a branch,
his sleepy eyes blinking.

Under the humped, rough bark,
beetle and aphid families creep.

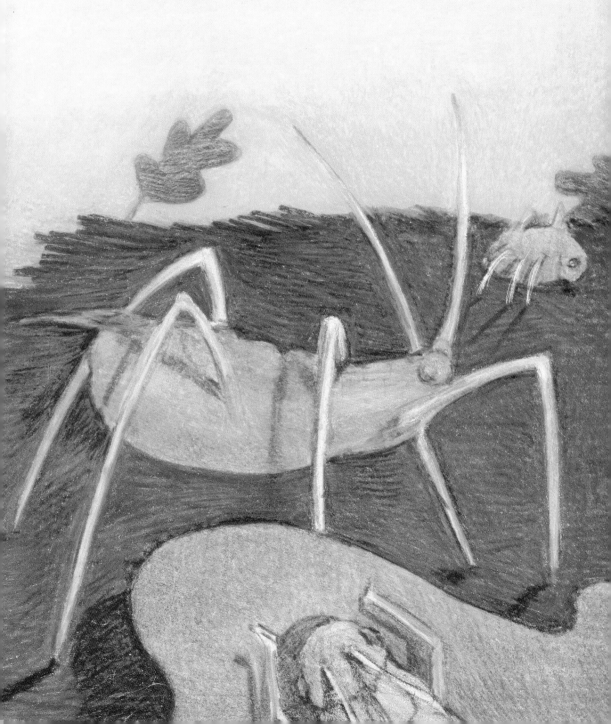

On the backs of leaves,
there are cocoon beds,
and butterflies
just coming out of their cocoons.

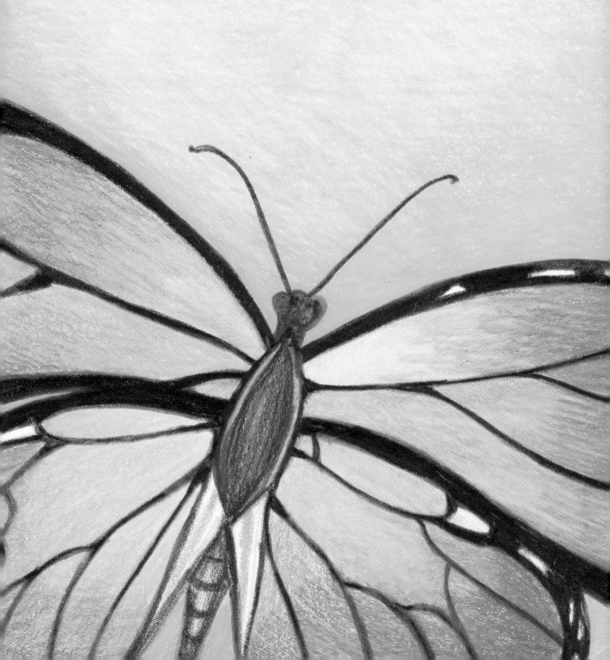

A skink
clings to his branch home
with five sticky, padded toes.

High up, inside the trunk of the tree,
is the home of the sly, masked, ring-tailed
raccoons.

And in the very tip top
of the grand, tall hideaway
apartment house tree,
there is a place
just for me.